NOW THAT YOU ARE BORN AGAIN WHAT'S NEXT?

PASTOR EMMANUEL ESSIEN

Now That You Are Born Again: What's Next?

Copyright @ 2020 Pastor Emmanuel Essien

ISBN: 9798574922613

All rights reserved.

This book is protected by the copyright laws of the United States of America.

This book may not be copied or reprinted for commercial gain or profit.

The use of short quotations or occasional page copying for personal or group study is permitted and encouraged.

Permission will be granted upon request.

Unless otherwise identified, scripture quotations are taken from The Holy Bible, King James Version.

This book is a Gift

From

To

Date

Now That You Are Born Again, What's Next?

Table Of Contents

Acknowledgment

Page vi

Introduction

Page 9

Chapter One

Understanding What It Means to Be Born Again

Page 11

Chapter Two

Water Baptism and Holy Ghost Baptism

Page 25

Chapter Three

The Authority of a Believer

Page 39

Chapter Four

The Gifts of the Spirit

Page 49

Chapter Five

The Fruit of the Spirit

Page 67

Chapter Six

Service in the Kingdom

Page 77

Acknowledgement

I use this forum to thank all my fellow co-laborers and burden bearers who had - over the 12 years of formal ministry here in the States - stood with us in Ministry as men raised by God, but who had first learned how to stand in His Presence.

To Revs Yinka and Rose Yusuf, our parents in the Lord of the Household of Love Church, Bishop and Rev Yomi and Esther Isijola of the Logos Ministries and Churches, Bishop and Prophetess Nuel and Derby Ikeakaman of the Freedom Ministries Int'l and Churches and Apostle and Pastor O.C and Edith Obikaram of the Christian

Fellowship World Outreach Church - all mentors in Ministry. I am grateful.

I also acknowledge Pastor Jeff Daniel of the Kingdom Light Church Int'l who has been a friend and encourager to get this book out.

I thank my parents, Dr E. S Essien(Late) and Mrs. Basseyawan Essien for all the values they taught us and for all the sacrifices made on our accounts for life (I honor you all), and most importantly my wife Prophetess Emem Essien and our children who have been there as help-meets and cheerleaders for all the challenges of life and Ministry - I salute and love you all.

Introduction

...GO THEREFORE AND MAKE DISCIPLES OF ALL NATIONS....

MATTHEW 28:19

This seems to be one of the least obeyed or ignored commandments of Christ by the Church today.

What we have today are people getting born again or saved without any proper teaching/training to make disciples out of these converts or new believers, and that has prompted this book with the hope and prayers that it would address this pertinent need of the church and to answer the questions of these new believers, so that they may be settled and established in their walk with God.

Understanding What It Means To Be Born Again

1

Understanding What It Means To Be Born Again

...HOW CAN A MAN BE BORN AGAIN
WHEN HE IS OLD...?
JOHN 3:4B

To answer Nicodemus' question we must first understand that man is a three part, or a tripartite being consisting of the spirit, soul, and body *(1 Thess 5: 23).* The question then becomes: which out of the three parts of man actually was born again? As far as Nicodemus understood, perhaps the man will have to go back to the mother's womb for a second time to be born again.

This learned religious man, who was supposed to know, undertook this line of reasoning because he only thought of man as just a body or physical being.

Now man is basically a spirit. In *Genesis 1:26* we are told that God said let us make man in our image and after our likeness, and in *John 4:24* we are told that God is a Spirit. This means that if God wanted to make man in His image and likeness He would have made man a spirit like Him. So, basically God created **ALL MEN** as spirit beings.

Now our bodies are simply the house that the spirit man lives in while on earth. Man was also given a mind or soul for self-expression or self-consciousness. So, the soul here consists of the mind, the memory, the intellect, the imagination, the will, the attitude or habit-forming center, and most importantly the decision-making center.

The question then is, what part of the man really got born again? And the answer is that it was the spirit of the man that was born again. Now you don't change height or complexion because you went to church one day and decided to give your life to Jesus. In fact, the things you have learned or the habits you formed before you became a Christian or born again - in most cases - remain the same after the born again experience.

To directly answer the question of how a man can be born again when he is old, Jesus said in *John 3:5* that except a man is born of (a) water and of the (b) Spirit he cannot enter into the kingdom of God.

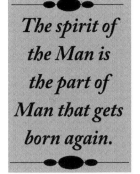
The spirit of the Man is the part of Man that gets born again.

SO, THE PROCESS for the born again experience involves these 2 things: WATER and the SPIRIT.

THE SPIRIT

Now starting with the Spirit, we must first

understand that after God created man good and without sin in the Garden of Eden, God also told man that the day man sins he will die! *(Gen 2:15-17, Romans 6:23)* So when man chose to side with the devil in complete disregard to God's commandment man died spiritually though he(man) was still walking around in the physical. (There was now a SEPARATION between God and man, as God by His nature is too holy to stand ONE SIN.)

For any man to now be accepted of God, his spirit must be born again by the Spirit of God *(John 3:6, Rom 8:9)* and that happened the day WE PRAYED AND ASKED JESUS TO COME INTO OUR LIVES.

So what really came into us instantaneously was the Spirit of Christ or the Spirit of God or the Holy Spirit (same Person) if we prayed in faith *(Romans 8:9)*. The bible also says that now our bodies are not only a house for our spirit man but also the house or temple of the Holy Spirit *(1 Corinthians 6: 19)*, and greater is He that is in us than he (the devil) that is in the world *(1 John 4:4).*

> **" *Now the born-again experience here is instantaneous if undertaken by faith.* "**

WATER

Water here refers to the power of the Word of God to affect or change a person.... *John 15:3*

Being born of water or the word is a process. For some it might be an elongated drag out process producing struggling, or unserious Christians who are not ready to pay the price of growing in the word *(1 Peter 2:2, Mat 4:4)*. For others, it is an intense purposeful process of getting into the word producing vibrant, maturing Christians who are not only on fire to get to know God's word but also live it out. *(Heb 5:12-14)*.

B} The Spiritual Implication of Being Born Again

...THEREFORE, IF ANY MAN BE IN CHRIST, HE IS A NEW CREATURE....

2 CORINTHIANS 5:17

The question is, what happens to a man who is now born again and invariably carries the Spirit of God in him *(2 Cor 5:17)*? How does that affect the man?

We will discuss briefly three areas of this man's life that can be affected now that he is a Christian or born again.

➔ He is now a new creature in Christ Jesus **(2 Cor 5:17)**

He has a new born again human spirit given birth to by the Spirit of God that now lives in him *(John 3:6)*, and as far as God is concerned he is not only forgiven but given a fresh and new start in Christ, with old things passing away *(including whatever he may have done before becoming a Christian)* and all things becoming new. And this is feasible because when God forgives a man the Bible says He takes our sins as far as the east is from the west *(Psalms 103:12)*.

New creation reality also implies that this man now has a new right standing with God (he is righteous) with all the benefits that come with having God not only as your Savior through Christ Jesus but also as your Father *(Mat 7:11).*

→ Secondly this Man can now be led by the Spirit of God *(Rom 8:14)*

This is so because the Spirit of God in the man *(received at new birth or when He became born again)* becomes the means or medium whereby God can now communicate with the man, depending on how sensitive his human spirit is to the Spirit of God *(this is called being "sensitive in the spirit").*

So often you hear of Christians saying that some voice on the inside of them seems to be telling them what to do or how to proceed - that voice in many cases could be the Voice of the Holy Spirit in you, trying to reach out to you or contact you through your spirit man. This is commonly called the "inner witness". This inner witness can be said to be the most common means for God to speak to His children who now carry His Holy Spirit in them.

So the level of your sonship is a function of or depends on how much you can hear and understand God, as there are sons and there are sons just as in the natural.

→ Thirdly this man is now empowered by the Holy Spirit in him to love as God loves ***(1 John 4:7-8)***

Now there are commonly three kinds of love. There is the **(a)** *Eros (*Greek word) from which we have the erotic, passionate, or physical love that exists between a man and a woman. There is also the (b) *Phileo* (Greek) or brotherly love, affection, friendship, or shared goodwill that exists among people with the same objective or goals, as in sports or at war fronts. Thirdly there is **(c)** *Agape* (another Greek word) that describes the God's unconditional love for mankind.

This is the one that we humans cannot exercise without the help of the Holy Spirit in us, since we are basically selfish in nature *(that is self first)* and would generally give love for a reason or with conditions.

So agape or God kind of unconditional love mentioned in ***1 John 4:7-8*** can only be expressed by the help of the Holy Spirit, which now lives in us as born again Christian ***(Rom 5:5-8, 1 Cor 13)***. That depends on how much you are willing to allow the Holy Spirit in you to run your affairs.

This is the kind of love that will make you pray and exercise goodwill for your enemies - as mentioned in

> *The Spirit of God in the man becomes the means whereby God can now communicate with the man.*

scriptures - and that by the help of the Holy Spirit that now lives in us as born again Christians.

C} Conclusion

In concluding this very important chapter about understanding what it means to be born again, I would like to point out that:

→ God now sees you as a new creature in Christ Jesus *(2 Cor 5:17)* and as His, He expects you to live worthy of Him (*1 Peter 2:9*) by the help of the Holy Spirit, whom we will talk more about in other chapters.

→ As a spiritually new or baby Christian, God, just like any parent, expects you to be responsible enough to want to grow spiritually by giving attention to His word through reading, studying, and giving deep thoughts (meditation) to His word and counsels, and fellowshipping with other believers in a local assembly, church, or fellowship group as iron sharpens iron, as the Bible says in ***Prov 27:17*** and also ***Heb 10:25.***

→ And lastly when we sin as Christians there is always room for forgiveness with our heavenly Father if only we are genuinely repentant of our sins *(**1 John 1:7-10**)*. That does not mean we take God for a fool or take God's grace and mercies for granted ***(Rom 6: 1-2).***

Water Baptism And Holy Ghost Baptism

2

Water Baptism And Holy Ghost Baptism

....'HERE IS WATER, WHAT STOPS ME FROM BEING BAPTIZED?'...

ACTS 8:36-37

1) What Is Water Baptism?

Water Baptism is a church ceremony, sacrament, or rite with spiritual implication used to symbolize the official initiation or admission of a believer into the church or the body of Christ.

It is something Jesus clearly commanded in *Mat 28:19.*

Jesus was also baptized in *Matthew 3:13-15* leaving us an example.

The word Baptism simply means to "dip in", or to immerse in water in this case, and in Christianity it becomes the formal indication by those being baptized that they want to be formally inducted or admitted into the church.

The ceremony can be done by an ordained minister or any born again Christian who understands what he or she is doing in the name of God the Father, Son, and the Holy Spirit.

It could be done in a stream, river, swimming pool or any body of water flowing or not, as long as it would allow for the complete immersion of the one to be baptized.

Baptism in itself cannot save, and as our text

indicates in *Acts 8:37,* it is only meant for those who have ALREADY believed that Jesus is the Son of God and has accepted Him as their Lord and Savior.

So one would still make heaven if he is born again but is unable to be baptized until right before his death, and in the same vein one could be baptized a hundred times and still miss heaven if such a person has never given his or her life to Christ, as we are saved by the finished work of Christ on the cross and not by water per se.

2) What Is The Spiritual Importance Of Water Baptism (What Does It Stand For?)

....KNOW YE NOT, THAT SO MANY OF US AS WERE BAPTIZED INTO JESUS CHRIST WERE BAPTIZED INTO HIS DEATH?...
ROMANS 6: 3-4

This scripture makes us understand that when a minister immerses the one to be baptized into water, it stands for our oneness with Jesus

Christ's death. Even as Christ died on the cross for our sins we also died with him (Paul says in ***Galatian 2:20***—*'I am crucified with Christ'....*) because it should have been us (for the wages of sin is death -- ***Romans 6:23)*** but He took our place.

> *Baptism in itself cannot save, it is only meant for those who have ALREADY believed that Jesus is the Son of God and has accepted Him as their Lord and Savior.*

The immersion in water also stand for our oneness with His burial ***(Romans 6:4)*** implying that when we come to Christ we are now dead to sin, our former way of living, and all that goes with it, just as ***2 Corinthians 5:17*** says that if any be in Christ he is a new creature: OLD THINGS ARE PASSED AWAY, and all things have become new.

So, a Christian who walks into that water now understands that he can leave behind or bury in that water by faith sins, habits, sickness, poverty, and everything that has no bearing in this, our new life in Christ Jesus.

The later part of **_Romans 6:4_** also says that like as Christ was raised from the dead by the glory of the Father, even so we also should walk in newness of life, implying that when you emerge from the water at baptism you are now one with His resurrection or newness of life in Christ Jesus.... with old things passed away, AND ALL THINGS BECOME NEW **_(2 Corinthians 5:17)_**.

It's like a man with another chance at life; forgiven and raised from the deadness of sin to a new life now in Christ Jesus. Amen!

B} Holy Ghost Baptism

......BUT YE SHALL RECEIVE POWER, AFTER THAT HOLY GHOST IS COME UPON YOU: AND YE SHALL BE WITNESSESS UNTO ME.......

ACTS 1:8

1) What Is Holy Ghost Baptism?

It is empowerment for service given to a born again Christian where the Holy Ghost comes upon the believer and he is energized to do service unto God (be my witness).

So, Jesus told His disciples that they should tarry (wait) in Jerusalem till they be endued with power from on high in *Luke 24:49,* and we see that promise made manifest in *Acts 2:1-4.*

2) Who Does The Baptism?

Jesus is the Baptizer of the Holy Spirit as in *Matthew 3:11*, and we need to ask Him in prayers for the Holy Ghost baptism as in *Luke 11:13.*

So we ask in faith, trusting that God will willingly give the Holy Ghost to as many as seek it from their hearts.

3) Does One Need To Seek For The Holy Bapstism After He's Born Again?

Yes, as shown in *Acts 19:1-7* where Paul met

certain disciples (or born again Christian) who had never heard of the Holy Ghost even though they were described as disciples.

Any believers that need empowerment for service would need the Holy Ghost baptism. This needs to be stressed because there are those who teach that once you are born again you are also baptized in the Holy Spirit, but from this scripture one can see that the disciples still needed to be baptize in the Holy Spirit.

4) Does One Have To Speak In Tongues After Being Baptized In The Holy Spirit?

Speaking in tongues or praying in the Holy Spirit is the common bible evidence that one is baptized in the Holy Spirit. We see this in the first instance of the Holy Ghost baptism in *Acts 2:4*, where the bible says that all the disciples were filled with the Holy Spirit and began to speak with other's tongues as the Holy Spirit enabled them (that is to say that it was not made up).

We see other instances in *Acts 10:45-47* and in *Acts 19:6-7* that go to show that the common proof of baptism of the Holy Spirit was speaking in tongues.

Now there could be other believers who are baptized in the Holy Spirit who may CHOOSE not to speak in tongues for many reasons, such as a lack of proper teaching/understanding on this subject, self-consciousness of speaking with your mouth what your mind does not understand, (because the bible says in *1 Cor 14:2* *—'ye that speaks in an unknown tongue speaks not unto men, but unto God: for no man* - including the speaker - understands him for in the spirit he speaks mysteries') and so forth. Nevertheless, the common evidence of baptism of the Holy Spirit is still speaking in tongues.

5) How Does One Get Baptized in The Holy Spirit?

First and foremost, you ask the Baptizer Jesus in prayers in English or whatever language you use *(Luke 11:13)*.

Secondly, you must ask in faith believing that God wants you to have the Holy Spirit (Luke 11:13) to be of more use to Him in your service.

Thirdly, you create an atmosphere of praise to create an atmosphere conducive for God's Presence as He delights in and inhabits the praises of His people *(Psalms 22:3)*. And as you continue to praise, ask and thank God among other things for the baptism of the Holy Spirit in your understanding.

Sooner or later you will discover a welling up or an urge in your inner being to start speaking or saying things other than the language you know or understand, if this has been handled correctly.

For many this becomes a challenge, because the conventional is to stop when you begin to verbalize things that your mind does not understand or initiate, and this is where you must be forewarned not to hesitate because the Bible says in *1 Corinthians 14:2* that *"he that speaks in unknown (or tongue not learned) speaks not unto men, but unto God: for no man (including you the speaker) understands him; however in the spirit he is speaking mysteries (unto God).*

So please, when that desire to speak foreign words comes up on your inside, don't STOP! For many have stopped here and would not proceed (even though the urge is there) to receive the fulness of the Holy Ghost baptism, as evidenced by speaking in tongue as in *Acts 2:4.*

> *Speaking in tongues or praying in the Holy Spirit is the common bible evidence that one is baptized in the Holy Spirit.*

However a word of caution here: do not pretend to speak in tongues if for any reason it doesn't arise naturally after you've prayed or you've been prayed for, for it's supposed to be as the Holy Spirit gives you utterance (or enables you to speak) as in *Acts 2:4.* Other hindrances to receiving Holy Ghost baptism with evidence of speaking in tongues could be: not enough or improper teaching on how to receive the Holy Ghost baptism, living in sin or sinful habits, unforgiveness or bitterness, unbelief or simply a choice not to, even though you should after you receive the Holy Ghost baptism *(Acts 2:4).*

6) EXAMPLES OF HOLY GHOST BAPTISM IN THE BIBLE

*The Holy Ghost Came Upon The Disciples - **ACTS 2:1-18***

*The Holy Ghost At Cornelius House - **ACTS 10:44-46***

*The Holy Ghost Given To The Disciples - **ACTS 19:1-7***

The Authority Of A Believer

3

The Authority Of
A Believer

Authority could be defined as Power or Right delegated or given. Delegation means to commit power, function, etc. to another as an agent or a deputy of the one that delegates.

So when God said in Genesis 1:26-28 *"let us make man in our image and after our likeness and let them have dominion"*, He was essentially saying let man represent me on earth as a governor or let man stand in my place.

Psalms 115:16 says that *"the heavens are the Lord's"* but the earth He has given to the children of men".

However, we see in *Genesis 3* how, through the deceit of the devil, man sinned against God by his disobedience to God's instruction and gave up this authority to the devil, who is now the god of this world system.

(2 Corinthians 4:4, Matthew 4:8-9).

But thank God for His Son Jesus because the story did not end there, as we are now through the sacrificial death of Jesus for our sins back to the place of authority in the name of Jesus.

And Jesus speaking in *Matthew 28:18-20* now says *"all power is given unto me in heaven and in earth. Go ye therefore and teach all nations, baptizing them in the NAME of the Father, and the Son, and the Holy Ghost".*

Phil 2:9-11 says that *God has exulted Jesus to the highest place and gave Him the name that is above every other name, so that at the mention of the name Jesus every knee should bow, of things in heaven, things on earth and things under the earth, and every tongue should confess the*

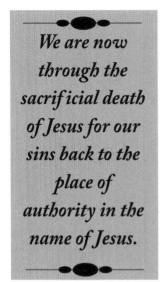

We are now through the sacrificial death of Jesus for our sins back to the place of authority in the name of Jesus.

Lordship of Jesus.

Jesus speaking in **Luke 10:19** says *"behold, I GIVE UNTO YOU POWER to tread on serpents and scorpions, and over all the power of the enemy: and nothing shall by any means hurt you".*

A) Our Authority As Christians Is Tied To Our Faith

1 John 5:4 says *"for whatsoever is born of God overcometh the world: and this is the victory that overcometh the world even our faith".*

That is to say that even though you are born again an overcomer, your overcoming is a function of (or is tied to) your faith. So, your faith in God and His word is a must if you will stand to exercise your authority as a child of God.

Now faith is not just believing God but acting on

what you believe, for faith without works (action) is dead *(James 2:17-18)*. If you are going to live this life as a child of God, and not just live but live with authority, then your faith must be in place *(Habakkuk 2:4)*. *Hebrews 10:38* says the just shall live by his faith.

Faith is also a fight, but it's a fight we will always win if we are willing to fight to enforce our authority as God's children. Paul writing to his son in the Lord, Timothy, says in *1 Timothy 6:12 "fight the good fight of faith....". And in 2 Timothy 4:7* he says "I have fought the good fight, I have finished my course, I have kept the faith" and Mat 11:12 says "from the days of John the Baptist until now the kingdom of heaven suffers violence and the violent take it by force".

We must be ready for this fight of faith if we will stand to enforce our authority, because our faith as God's children will be tested or tried as in *James 1:3,* where it says *"the TRYING OF YOUR FAITH works or develops perseverance"* and *1 Peter 1:7* says *"THE TRIAL OR TESTING OF YOUR FAITH, being much more precious than of gold that perisheth, though it be tried with fire, might be found unto praise and honor and glory at the* appearing of Jesus Christ".

B) The Scope Of Authority For A Believer

What is the limit of our authority as God's children? The Bible speaking in **Genesis 1:26** says "....*let them have dominion or authority over the fish of the sea, and over the fowl of the air, and over the cattle, and over all the earth, and over every creeping thing that creepeth upon the earth*"----so the scope of our authority encompasses all of nature be it in the air, in the sea, or on the land. We see a display of this in **Joshua 10:12** when Joshua spoke to the sun and asked it to stand still (not to go down or dark) until they were done with the war they were engaged in. Also, we see in **Acts 28:3-5** how a poisonous snake bit apostle Paul and he came to no harm.

Mark 16:17-18 also makes us understand that we have authority over devils or demons, over sickness, and if we drink any deadly things or poisons (unknowingly) it shall not hurt us.

C) Conclusion

And as we stand to enforce our given authority as God's children, we must learn to stand strong in the power of God and His might and not our own, as we have none except what we have been given. We must also stand strong to enforce our authority fully decked with the weapon of warfare that God has given us for this fight as prescribed in ***Ephesians 6:10-18.***

The Gifts Of The Spirit

The Gifts Of The Spirit

Paul in his writing to the church at Corinth in 1 Corinthians 12:1-11 (which will be our main scripture of reference) talked about the 9 gifts of the Holy Spirit, primarily given to the church or to us as God's children to benefit, help, and prosper in the work of the church/ministry as mentioned in *1 Corinthians 12:7.*

Paul began in *1 Cor 12:1* by writing on how many seem so ignorant of these spiritual gifts.

There are 9 gifts of the Spirit as mentioned in *1 Cor 12: 8-10*, all empowered by the same Holy

Spirit who gives different gifts to each person as He wishes.

The 9 gifts could be group into
a) Revelation gifts
b) Utterance gifts and
c) Power gifts.

A) Revelation Gifts make it possible for the Holy Spirit to bring to light/reveal that which has been hidden or which ordinarily would have remained unknown.

This includes Word of wisdom, Word of knowledge and Discerning of spirits.

B) Utterance Gifts involve speaking and include the Gift of Prophecy, Gift of tongues, and Interpretation of tongues.

C) Power Gifts demonstrate the manifestation of the power of God and include the Gift of Faith, Gifts of healing, and Working of miracles.

REVELATION GIFTS
1) Word of Wisdom

Wisdom is the application of knowledge. While information or knowledge may be available, knowing what to do in difficult cases can only take place with the empowerment/gifting of the Holy Spirit.

This has nothing to do with studies or experience.

For example, the case in ***1 Kings 3:16-28*** where two women laid a claim to one child, which is of course impossible since the two women could not possibly be the mothers of a single child at the same time, but that was the available information (knowledge). It only took the gift of God's wisdom which King Solomon had earlier asked for and received from God in ***1 Kings 3:3-12*** to come to the proper judgement of how to handle the case.

Another instance is in ***Acts 15:1-22.***
We are told in ***Acts 15:1*** that certain men in the

early church were insisting that one could not really be saved unless he was circumcised according to the law of Moses after he becomes a Christian, and there was much disputing and contention over this, especially from those in the Sect of the Pharisees who also believed in circumcision. The matter was brought before the church leadership in Jerusalem.

Here again there is information (knowledge) of a problem on the ground but it was challenging to know how to go about resolving it until James, who was the Pastor then of the church in Jerusalem, began to speak the wisdom of God in *Acts 15:13-22*. It pleased all sides of the argument and brought a settlement to a thorny issue that would have possibly caused a major rift in the early church.

2) Word of Knowledge

This is the Holy Spirit giving you specific information about a situation that you would not ordinary have known by any means.

There are many ways the Holy Spirit does this,

but this has to do with your specific dealings with Him as we grow in this gifting and especially in our sensitivity to Him.

In *John 4:7-19* is the story of the woman of Samaria and her interaction with Jesus. In verse 17 of this scripture Jesus asked the woman to go call her husband, only for the woman to respond that she had no husband. Jesus responded that she was being truthful because she had five husbands. There was no way Jesus would have had such knowledge or information except that it was revealed to Him by the Holy Spirit.

3) Discerning of spirits

This is the ability to recognize and distinguish between the Spirit of God and other spirits.

It is a supernatural insight by the Holy Spirit to know what spirit is at work, especially in the manifestation of the supernatural.

In *Acts 16:16-19* is the account of a young lady who had the spirit of divination. That is to say she had the ability to discover hidden knowledge

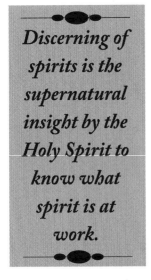

Discerning of spirits is the supernatural insight by the Holy Spirit to know what spirit is at work.

but by the means of spirits other than the Spirit of God or the Holy Spirit.

In the story she was able to provide the right information about Paul and his team and the reason they were in town, but she did so by using the wrong spirit. The Bible tells us this went on for many days, until Paul under the direction of the Holy Spirit was able to see into the spirit realm and was able to determine that even though she was saying the right things, she was not doing so by the Spirit of God.

Now *1 John 4:1-3* gives us a general guideline to try or test the spirit at work, whether it be of God or not. It hinges on the fact that every spirit that confesses that Jesus is come in the flesh or as human is from God, and every spirit that does not confess that Jesus is come in the flesh is not from God. So, this the general rule of the thumb.

UTTERANCE GIFTS

1) Gift Of Prophecy

Prophecy, particularly in the Old Testament, had to do with being able to foretell the future by the Spirit of God at work in the men or women of God. The proof that one is a true prophet is when a message that supposedly came from God comes to pass. See **2 Peter 1:20-21 and Hebrews 1:1**.

However, in the New Testament prophecies also include the proper handling of scripture to build, exhort. and comfort **(1 Cor 14:1-3)**.

So a Prophet stands as one in contact with God by His Spirit and is able to hear from God and to speak on His behalf, serving as a go-between for God and humanity by delivering messages or teaching from Him directly as he hears it from the Lord or His word.

I must also throw in a word of caution here that no prophet could ever claim to hear from God anything that could be said to be contrary to the scripture, because the bible has also been described as a more sure word of prophecy in *2 Peter 1:19*. Secondly, *2 Timothy 3:16* states that all scripture is breathed out by God or given by divine inspiration.

2) Gift Of Tongues

This is more than just the ability to speak in tongues as expected of believers. As the Bible says in *Mark 16:17:* this signs shall follow them that believes; in my name they shall speak with new tongues...(this is the personal prayer language if you chose to pray in the spirit).

However, in the gift of tongues one with this grace or gifting by the Holy Spirit speaks or prays in tongues to and on behalf of a congregation to God. One could also be empowered by the Holy Spirit to speak in the language of men or others, especially for the work of the kingdom or to evangelize.

For the gift of tongues to be useful and of benefit one must also pray for interpretation of tongues, because the Bible says in *1 Cor 14:1* that "he that speaks in an unknown tongues speaks not unto men but unto God: for no man (including the speaker) understand what he is saying (except he has or someone else in the congregation that has the gift of interpretation of tongues) because in the spirit he speaks mysteries to God".

3) Interpretation Of Tongues

This is the supernatural enablement by the Holy Spirit to express a response from God in an intelligible language to an unknown tongue spoken by one with the gift of tongues.

This is actually a two-way conversation/traffic where one prays mysteries to God in tongues and another or the same individual with the gift of Interpretation of tongues gets a response from God to the tongue that was spoken to the benefit of the congregation.

I must however caution here that interpretation of tongues is not the same as translation of tongues.

Power Gifts
1) Faith

Every child of God has some degree of faith. For you cannot possibly be a Christian without enough faith to even believe in Jesus whom you have never seen. Therefore, the Bible says in **Romans 12:3** that *God has dealt to every man the measure of faith.*

However, there are some in the church, especially 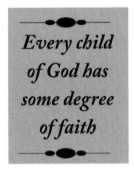 those in the place of authority or leadership, who seem to have a higher dimension of the grace of faith as enabled by the Holy Spirit. You hear them make pronouncement and take steps that the average Christian would not make as empowered by the Holy Spirit. They have to have this degree of faith to be able to give a sense of direction to the rest of the church, especially when in leadership positions.

We see faith on display when Elijah the prophet had to confront the over 400 prophets of Baal, and asked the fire of God to come down after he had requested that water be poured on the same burnt offering, thus proving the God that answers by fire.

Today we have great men and women of faith doing exploits for God and for the kingdom, but the bottom line remains that even though this special grace for faith is as empowered by the Holy Spirit, faith still comes by hearing the Word of God. One that would flow in this grace must be one given to God's word, not just in knowing it but in living it out.

2) Gifts Of Healing

This is different from the general expectation that as believers the bible says we shall lay hands on the sick and they shall recover *(Mark 16:18).*

There are some that God has placed in the Church who are empowered by the Holy Spirit with the special grace to heal all kinds of diseases, no matter the disease.

It's called gift(s) of healing because in terms of operation some may be called to deal with certain areas of healing in the body or mind, and through experience as governed by the Holy Spirit seem more attuned or adjusted to that area of healing compared to others.

For example, over time some may see more cripples healed in their Ministry compared to diseases like blindness or cancer. Though this may also be affected by your location and the specific healing needs depending on where you are at that point in time.

But whatever may be the case, the blood of Jesus fully paid for any diseases, and it is just for us to discover the areas of our calling and their operation as determined by the Lord and empowered by the Holy Spirit.

3) Working Of Miracles

This has to do with any supernatural manifestations as empowered by the Holy Spirit to demonstrate the power of God, so that what would have taken a natural course of events supernaturally results in a different outcome.

Healing could, for example, be a form of a miracle, but not all miracles have to do with healing. When Joshua commanded the moon and the sun to stand still at Gibeon ***(Joshua 10:12-13)*** so that he and his army may continue fighting in daylight, that was a miracle. When Jesus turned water into wine at the wedding in Cana, that was also a miracle ***(John 2: 1-11)***.

There also are some whom God has placed in the church to perform all kinds of miracles as empowered by the Holy Spirit.

IN CONCLUSION

For one to see any of these gifts made manifest in their lives as Christians it's important to cultivate a relationship with the Holy Spirit, as all the gifts are empowered by Him and are manifested through Him. One does this by being mindful of His person in terms of what pleases or offends Him. The Bible speaking in ***Ephesians 4:30*** says grieve not the Holy Spirit...so one can't live a life that brings Him grief or displeasure and at the same time turn to expect the gifting of the Spirit from Him.

Secondly, we must check our motivation for the giftings of the Holy Spirit; which has to be love. This is the more excellent way to receive the gifts of the Holy Spirit *(1 Corinthians 12:31 and 1 Corinthians 13).*

Lastly, one must covet or earnestly desire these giftings of the Holy Spirit *(1 Corinthians 12:31)* with faith in your heart knowing that it is what God the father wants for His Children and for the work of the kingdom here on Earth *(Luke 11:13).*

The Fruit Of The Spirit

5

The Fruit Of The Spirit

The fruit of the Spirit here refers to what ought to be the byproduct of the Holy Spirit indwelling a believer or in the life of a Christian. It's the influence of the Holy Spirit in the life or behavior of a Christian made manifest in the day to day lifestyle of a believer. *Matthew 7:16 says "ye shall know them by their fruits...."*

The fruit is referenced here as if it were singular, even though there are nine listed here by Apostle Paul in our key scripture of *Galatian 5:16-25,* because they are all from one source: the Holy Spirit indwelling a Christian.

> *The fruit of the Spirit is the influence of the Holy Spirit in the life of a Christian made manifest in the day to day lifestyle of a believer.*

So, we will be looking at the nine fruit of the Spirit as mentioned in **Galatian 5:22-23** by defining and explaining them and how they can be borne in the life of a believer.

A) Love

Love here refers to agape - the God kind of unconditional love that could only be borne by the help of the Holy Spirit indwelling a Christian *(1 John 4: 7-8)* since we are all by nature selfish. That is to say, we will look out for ourselves and our interests first before anyone else except by the help of the Holy Spirit (***Romans 5: 5,8)***.

B) Joy

This is happiness not dependent on circumstances *(James 1:2)* as empowered by the

Holy Spirit in the life of a Christian. The convention is for one to be happy when things are good and obviously behave differently when things are not going well. That is to say, a Christian, by the help and in relationship with the Holy Spirit, can exhibit the Joy of the Lord irrespective of the circumstances being empowered by the Holy Spirit. ***Nehemiah 8:10*** says *"the joy of the Lord is my strength"* and *Jesus endured the cross* in ***Hebrews 12:2*** *"for the joy set before Him"*.

C) Peace

This is a state of being still, or a state of harmony or freedom from commotion, strife, annoyance, or anxiety irrespective of what is going on around you by the working of the Holy Spirit in you. It is the peace of God *(John 14:27)* that surpasses what your common sense or understanding tells you *(Phil 4:7).*

D) Longsuffering

As the name implies, it is a state of suffering long, forbearance, or being very patient with others by the help of the Holy Spirit living in you.

Apostle Paul in his writing in **Romans 9:22-24** talks about how God endured with much longsuffering toward vessels of wrath fitted for destruction, to show forth the richness or the magnitude of His mercies.

E) Gentleness

To be tame, polite, refined (as we say "Gentlemen") or have a moral integrity by the working of the Holy Spirit in the life of a Christian. It is also being kind, amiable or friendly, sociable, or good natured. A state of being moderate and agreeable.

2 Tim 2:24-25 says, *"the servant of the Lord must not strive, but be gentle unto all men, apt to teach, patient"*. We see here how the fruit of gentleness or being approachable is also a requirement to be an effective teacher to others.

James 3:17 says "but the wisdom that is from

above is first pure, then peaceable, GENTLE, and EASY TO BE ENTREATED, full of mercy and good fruits".

F) Goodness

Goodness is a state of moral excellence or uprightness, or something in a high quality or excellent condition.

Jesus stated clearly in **Mark 10:18** that none is good himself or herself except for God. So for one to be good, a state which is commonly judged by our actions *(Col 1:10)*, can only be by God's Spirit. That is why this is also qualified as one of the fruits of the Spirit.

G) Faith

This is the character trait that outlines our dependability and trust in God based on our confidence in God and His faithfulness to us as God.

The Bible makes it clear that everyone born of

God's Spirit has some degree of faith *(Romans 12:3).*

H) Meekness

Meekness could be defined as strength under control or to be tamed (like in wild animals) by the help of the Holy Spirit. Meekness could be viewed as the opposite of self-assertiveness or self-interest *(Gal. 6:1).*

It is not to be seen as a weakness *(Mat 11:29)* but rather a very important key ingredient to promoting unity and peace, especially within the body of Christ or the Church.

The meek are teachable, the meek can have it all in life and do not have to show it off, all by the help of the Holy Spirit in the life of a believer.

I) Temperance

Also called self-control, where through the help of the Holy Spirit we have strength to say "no" to our fleshy desires *(Gal 5:16)* and "yes" to the Holy

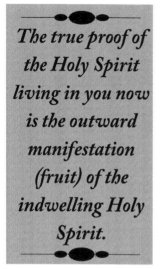

The true proof of the Holy Spirit living in you now is the outward manifestation (fruit) of the indwelling Holy Spirit.

Spirit. It also speaks of self-control to our body and its sensual appetites, and desires all by the help of the Holy Spirit and as the fruit of the Holy Spirit.

It also talks of being moderate in all things ***(Phil 4:5).***

Now in Conclusion

We can say that the true proof of the Holy Spirit (seed) living in you now as a child of God is the outward manifestation (fruit) of the indwelling Holy Spirit. Let us also remember that even though we all potentially have the Holy Spirit in us as God's children, it is still up to us to yield to/allow the working of God's Spirit in our inside ***(Gal 6:16)*** for this outward manifestation called the fruit of the Spirit.

Service In The Kingdom

6

Service In The Kingdom

This is the ultimate reason for our being born again and left here on earth, even though heaven is our final home for eternity with the Lord. In other words, we are saved to serve or to represent God here on earth as His children now born of the Holy Spirit.

Key Text: *Luke 19: 12-26*

A) Requirement for Service

The main requirement for Service is one being faithful or committed *(1 Cor 4:2)* to what we are called to do in God's kingdom, visibly represented here on earth as the Church, especially the local

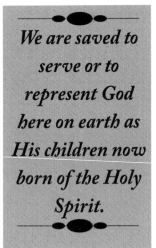

We are saved to serve or to represent God here on earth as His children now born of the Holy Spirit.

Church you are involved with. This begins with your availability, or giving yourself to service to God, because God is not looking for the qualified but the available who He can qualify. We should give ourselves in whatever capacity we can right now (see the story of the Woman with the Alabaster box of ointment in **Mark 14:3-8** whom Jesus commended as having done what she could). It is not about what you can do, but rather how well before God you are doing what He has given you to do at this point in time.

B) Importance of Belonging to a Local Church

→ For fellowship with other Christians so as to be fed with God's word, that you may grow spiritually now that you are born again (see **Heb 10:25).**

→ Constant fellowship and the Word will also strengthen or build up (edify), encourage (or exhort), and comfort you in your walk with God.

→ Church also means a place where you have placed yourself under some supervision and accountability, especially as a growing Christian.

→ Lastly, you put yourself in a position where you are plugged in to receive, and you are also opportuned to be of service to God and His kingdom through the local church that you are involved with.

C) Getting Involved

After joining a church it's important to submit yourself to the local church authority by introducing yourself either directly to the Pastor or any sub-head, depending on the church structure. Also inquire as to where you could be of service, remembering again that it is not about what you do but how faithful you are in what you are called to do.

Most churches have departments that one could get involved with, like the ushering, the technical, the Praise and worship Team or the Choir, the children's department, the intercessory or prayer group, and many more.

D) Benefits of Service In The Kingdom (Local Church)

→ It helps your personal growth and maturity in the matters of God, as you are trained more or less on the job as you get involved with God and His Church.

→ It creates a sense of belonging and fellowship as you serve along with other believers in the church.

→ Just as in the story of the parable of talents (in *Luke 19:12-26)* service also brings promotion and reward in life here on earth and in the life to come *(Luke 18: 28-30).*

→ Service also brings a distinction in life between those who serve God and those don't *(Mal 3:14-18).*

IN CONCLUSION

My prayer for you is that He who began a good work in you will perfect all that concerns you, as you choose daily to put first the welfare of the kingdom of God above all. I also pray that you will soon discover that God is a Rewarder of them who diligently seek Him.

May God bless you and your new life in Christ, may you grow daily and have a greater sense of fulfilment of living especially for Him by His grace, and that as He promised in His word that nothing can ever separate you from the love He has for you *(Romans 8:31-39).*

WELCOME AGAIN TO THE FAMILY.

Made in the USA
Middletown, DE
27 November 2022